Free But Not Delivered

Free But Not Delivered

Franklin Depp

Free, but Not Delivered
Trilogy Christian Publishers A Wholly Owned Subsidiary of Trinity Broadcasting Network
2442 Michelle Drive Tustin, CA 92780

Printed in the USA.
Rights Department, 2442 Michelle Drive, Tustin, CA 92780.

For information about special discounts for bulk purchases, please contact Trilogy Christian Publishing.

Manufactured in the United States of America
10 9 8 7 6 5 4 3 2 1
Library of Congress Cataloging-in-Publication Data is available.
ISBN: 978-1-64773-086-4
E-ISBN: 978-1-64773-087-1

Dedication

To my wife, Shelly Depp, thank you for your commitment and your tenacity. You have always been my number-one cheerleader, encouraging me to keep moving forward through the trials and tribulations. You believed in me when I did not believe in myself. I dedicate this book to you for being an awesome woman of God. To my children—Antonio, Maurice, Marque, Marlik, Markel, Marchaja, and Lachaja—thank you for all of your love and patience through the process. To God be the glory!

In loving memory of Beverly Jean Depp
Siblings: Teresa Depp, Johnnie Depp, Joynita Houston

Contents

Introduction

As Christians, our freedom comes through Jesus Christ, and His death and resurrection. I was bought with a price. The shedding of Jesus Christ's blood gives me access to the throne of grace. It's not that I deserve it, but the price has already been paid, because God sent His only Son for this reason:

For God so loved the world, that he gave his only begotten Son, that whosoever believeth in him should not perish, but have everlasting life.

—John 3:16

I no longer walk by the authority of the old sin master, but I am now under the new ownership of Jesus Christ. Galatians 5:1 tells us this: "*It is for freedom that Christ has set us free. Stand firm, then, and do not let yourselves be burdened again by a yoke of slavery*" (NIV). Since we live here on earth and Satan and his fallen angels live here on earth as well, Satan has tried to bring my mind back into captivity, so I can live as if I have never been saved from sin. So many of us as Christians are being used by the enemy, and we don't realize it, because we are so caught up with the cares of this world.

We have lost focus on the attack of our minds, and we have found ourselves doing things and saying things that we should not do or say as a Christian. This is why, until we recognize who we are and whose we are in Christ, we will continue to walk as slaves with freedom papers, never coming to enjoy or rejoice or give God praise for what He has done. We should always give the Lord praise.

God sees us as free people. John 8:36 states, "*If the Son therefore shall make you free, ye shall be free indeed.*" My spirit is free, but my flesh is the old slave master. I have discovered that I must feed one and starve the other, and which one you decide to feed will lead your life, whether it be the Spirit of God unto obedience (your true freedom) or the old slave master (the flesh, which will bring you back to bondage, or Egypt.

In Galatians 5:16, Paul wrote, "*This I say then, walk in the spirit, and ye shall not fulfill the lust of the flesh*" (NIV). It is a choice we have to make every day of our lives. Some days will be more challenging than other days, but if we rely on the Holy Spirit, we can be victorious every time. But we must submit our ways and thoughts to the things of God, so we can resist the devil, because the enemy does not want anything to do with the God of heaven. The devil knows he is no challenge to God. That's why it is very important that we walk in obedience to Christ.

There are millions of Christians who are living an undelivered life, because we have lost our Christian identity, and we must take back what the enemy has stolen from us. First Samuel 30:8 tells us: "*And David inquired at the LORD, saying, Shall I pursue after this troop? shall I overtake them? And he answered him, Pursue: for thou shalt surely overtake them, and without fail recover all.*" It is time for the people of God to recover it all. Everything that God has promised us through Jesus Christ is still ours, but we must put off the slavery of depression, the slavery of hate, the slavery of fear, the slavery of insecurity, and the slavery of jealousy, and we must put on mercy, love, peace, joy, forgiveness, and long-suffering.

Ephesians 4:22–24 tells us "*to put off your old self, which belongs to your former manner of life and is corrupt through deceitful desires, and to be renewed in the spirit of your mind, and to put on the new self, created after the likeness of God in true righteousness and holiness.*" The enemy wants us to believe his lies of deception. Satan's strategy is to get us to believe that we are not free. He also wants us to believe that we have no hope, that we will never be anything. It's all a lie. One thing that Satan cannot change is what God did through Jesus Christ on Calvary's cross two thousand years ago. Your victory is forever completed in Jesus Christ.

Now, because Satan can't change what God has done, his ultimate goal is to change you, to get you to believe the lies of deception. He will even go so far as to camouflage himself to fit in. He will try to enslave us with the work of God and keep us from accessing the promises of God. The only way that we can see the enemy's strategy is by studying the Word of God daily. Again, in John 8:32 Jesus said, "*Ye shall know the truth, and the truth shall make you free.*"

The enemy wants the saints to dwell on what we used to be (sinners), but the grace of God now allows us to be who God has called us to be—victorious and righteous. The Bible lets us know that the devil is the father of lies, but it also gives us a clear understanding of whether we are free or walking in the slavery of the enemy's blindfold of deception. In John 8:44, Jesus said, "*Ye are of your father the devil, and the lusts of your father ye will do. He was a murderer from the beginning, and abode not in the truth, because there is no truth in him. When he speaketh a lie, he speaketh of his own: for he is a liar, and the father of it.*" God sent His Son so that we do not have to walk in the enemy's lies.

Through Christ, we are the righteousness of God, not through any righteousness of our own, but totally through Christ's righteousness. How can I be righteous when I struggle as a Christian? The Bible says that we will all have trials and tribulations. In John 16:33, Jesus said, "*These things I have spoken unto you, that in me ye might have peace. In the world ye shall have tribulation: but be of good cheer; I have overcome the world.*"

Your struggle does not determine your righteousness, because your righteousness is of Jesus Christ. It is not based on your own works, but on grace, faith, and your belief in Christ Jesus. What gets Christians in trouble is that we listen to the lies of Satan, telling us that we are not good enough, and then we find ourselves trying to work our way to be right with God. Denominations and names on church buildings will not make you right with God. You will never be righteous through your own ability. Second Timothy 1:9 says, "*Who hath saved us and called us with an holy calling, not according to our works, but according to his own purpose and grace, which was given to us in Christ Jesus before time began.*" I'm not working to be free; I'm working because I am free and because God has called me with a holy calling. We must be devoted to the service of God.

1

THE WILDERNESS

The children of Israel were enslaved for over 425 years, and then God set the children of Israel free from slavery in Egypt—over a million people. God sent Israel into the wilderness, where the children of Israel adopted the spirit of complaining. This spirit is very dangerous. The reason I say that is because of the words of Philippians 2:14–16: "*Do everything without grumbling or arguing, so that you may become blameless and pure, children of God without fault in a warped and crooked generation. Then you will shine among them like stars in the sky as you hold firmly to the word of life. And then I will be able to boast on the day of Christ that I did not run or labor in vain.*"

The children of Israel were misrepresenting the calling of God on their lives. God inhabits the praises of His people. Israel should have adopted the spirit of praise, because when praises go up, the blessings come down. The wilderness was a place for transformation: Israel needed to get acquainted with their God so they could know their identity in God. Israel was having an identity crisis. The Israelites did not know who they were in God. The enemy will always fight you over your identity. Luke 4:3 tells us: "*The devil said to him [Jesus], If you are the Son of God, tell this stone to become bread.*" And the devil said to Jesus in Matthew 4:6, "*If you are the Son of God…throw yourself down. For it is written: He will command his angels concerning you, and they will lift you up in their hands, so that you will not strike your foot against a stone.*" Anytime the devil causes you to wonder who you are in God, you'll fall for anything. We will never receive anything from God if we do not know our identity in Him. The enemy uses his sneaky strategy of doubt and deception. He knows that once you lie down or give up your birthright, your God-given authority, it will be easy for him to execute his plan. Saints, remember that in John 10:10, Jesus said, "*The thief comes only to steal and kill and destroy.*"

But ye are a chosen generation, a royal priesthood, an holy nation, a peculiar people; that ye should shew forth the praises of him who hath called you out of darkness into his marvellous light. Which in time past were not a people, but are now the people of God: which had not obtained mercy, but now have obtained mercy.

—1 Peter 2:9–10

When God is developing us to come higher, it seems to our flesh that we are being neglected or that God does not care. But God freed Israel out of Egypt and granted Israel the physical liberty for which they had been praying. God was doing something much more remarkable than giving them physical freedom; God's next task was to bring Israel out of Egypt spiritually. God knew that He could not put new wine in old wineskins; Israel began to complain, accusing Moses of bringing them out in the wilderness to kill them. Israel was right to a certain extent: God was trying to kill off their mentality, not their physicality. We can see that the first thing that God and Moses had to deal with was the people complaining.

It was just like we are today in the twenty-first century: God cannot take us into the Promised Land with a slave mentality. We are free but not delivered. There are things in our lives that we must change, and we must repent of our sin with the help of the Holy Spirit before we can proceed in God's master plan for our lives. The wilderness was a place for Israel to detox, to purge themselves from idol worship, from physical abuse, and from verbal abuse—from, to sum up in three words, *SIN*. It is a sad thing to be blessed and not to recognize it. The reason Israel could not see how blessed they were was because they never reverenced God for who He was: He is the God of the universe, the God of all creation.

The people of God have to realize that God can change anything at any time, no matter what the circumstance. He is God, and there is no one like Him. Stop looking at what you see and start preparing for what God has said will take place. What you see now is a distraction of what God said. Everything that does not line up with what God said is a distraction to your destiny. When God communicates to your spirit through your dreams, or through the prophets, to the natural eye it will never line up with your circumstances. God always gives you a preview of your destiny.

When God sent the twelve spies to investigate the Promised Land, ten of the spies came back with a negative report, and only two came back with a positive report. All of the spies saw the same thing, but they did not perceive it in the same way. Why? Ten of the spies were looking at taking the Promised Land in their own strength and their own insight, and their fear and emotion took hold. The other two spies, Joshua and Caleb, were looking at taking the Promised Land in God's strength and through the Word of God and faith. Romans 10: 17 tells us that "*faith comes by hearing and hearing by the word of God.*" Stop procrastinating and move! I know what you are about to say: "I do not have any money, but God said to move; I have no support, but God said to move." Moving means making preparations for your destiny. Stop wasting time. Procrastination is like trying to drive your car in neutral. You have the potential and hope and big dreams and the promises of God, but the only thing that's stopping you is that you have not put your dreams and the promises of God in drive!

That generation took the promises of God to their graves, not because the promises were not theirs, but because they didn't believe that it was theirs. Do not take your dreams and your promises from God to the grave. God has given you dreams to impact your generation and your children's children. Proverbs 13:22 tells us, "*A good man leaves an inheritance to his children's children, and the wealth of the sinner is stored up for the righteous*" (NASB).

2

Faith without Works Is Dead

What does it profit, my brethren, if someone says he has faith but does not have works? Can faith save him? If a brother or sister is naked and destitute of daily food, and one of you says to them, "Depart in peace, be warmed and filled," but you do not give them the things which are needed for the body, what does it profit ? Thus also faith by itself, if it does not have works, is dead. But someone will say, "You have faith, and I have works." Show me your faith without your works, and I will show you my faith by my works. You believe that there is one God. You do well. Even the demons believe—and tremble! But do you want to know, O foolish man, that faith without works is dead? Was not Abraham our father justified by works when he offered Isaac his son on the ground altar? Do you see that faith was working together with his works, and by works faith was made perfect? And the Scripture was fulfilled which says, "Abraham believed God, and it was accounted to him for righteousness." And he was called the friend of God. You see then that a man is justified by works, and not by faith only.

—James 2:14–24 NKJV

The children of Israel wanted the promise of God, but they did not want to go through the process of securing the promise. The Israelites were excited about the ideal of change, but they were not excited about the process of change. What I mean is that the children of Israel were excited about coming out of Egypt, but they were not excited about Egypt coming out of them. The enemy did not mind Israel hearing from God; he just didn't want Israel to believe and to change, to figure out who they were in God. God did not just want Israel to hear and see what He said, but He wanted them to respond. However, fear will cause you to try to figure it out before going out, but faith causes you to go out before you figure it out. Fear will cause us to miss our "God opportunity"; that generation missed their promise and their promotion.

There were three things that stopped Israel from receiving the Promised Land. The first is a *negative attitude*; the second is *fear*; and the third is *unbelief*. Israel is God chosen people. It is the same with Christians today. We complain to God about how we are going to pay for things, how we can do things, when are certain things going to happen, what are we going to do?

As Christians, we all have said similar things at certain times in our life, but complaining is a sign that we are frustrated with where we are presently and with the condition in which we find ourselves, but if we look at history, complaining did not get Israel out of the wilderness—and it will not get you out of your situation, either. Complaining only gives your enemy an advantage to delay you from your destiny. If we don't learn from history, we will repeat it again. Learn how to use your mouth to your advantage.

The problem with today's Christians is that we use our mouths to speak our circumstances and our feelings. Yes, I understand that our circumstances don't always line up with our promises, but no matter what the circumstances, you must speak out your promise (speak life!). I have fallen into the same situation myself. God never intended for us to get complacent or adapted to our wilderness circumstances. God brought me out of the slavery of the hood, and now I'm in my wilderness

The wilderness is a place of testing in development. It is just like what happens in any car company: Everything that they create and develop, before it leaves the manufacturer, it first must be tested. I will give you another analogy, the university of the wilderness. Any university that you attend will require you to learn the material and be tested on it. The testing is to see if you are prepared for the next level, to move forward. If you think you are going to get the promise without encountering problems, you have been deceived by the enemy. The problem is actually an indication that you are closer to your destiny than you think. Proverbs 3:5–7 advises us to "*trust in the* L*ORD with all thine heart; and not unto thine own understanding; in all thy ways acknowledge him, and he shall direct thy paths. Be not wise in thine own eyes: fear the* L*ORD, and depart from evil.*" Remember this: God will never give you a vision without His provision. God would never have let you see it if it wasn't yours to have. Don't let the residue of your past keep you from the possibilities of today.

3

Generational Curses

Generational curses have been broken through Jesus Christ, but the enemy has been deceiving Christians, illegally causing them to believe his lies. Christians are no longer under the slavery of their forefathers' past sins, but for unbelievers this not so. Unbelievers will walk in their forefathers' curses as if they were normal. Until an unbeliever receives Christ, that is the way it will be for them, but Jesus died for the whole world. I know you have heard this before: "He is just like his father," or "She is just like her mother."

The enemy is keeping the same cycle throughout generations and generations. These are some things that he uses to keep you in bondage: drugs, alcohol, tobacco, fornication, adultery, disobedience, lying, greed, homosexuality, arrogance, pride, selfishness, backbiting, unforgivness, self-righteousness, suicide, fear, murder, division, prejudice, depression, bitterness, and anger. But with a Christian, the enemy strategically tries to deceive us and cause us to walk in the curse blindly.

First Peter 5:8 advises us to "*be sober, be vigilant; because your adversary the devil, as a roaring lion, walketh about, seeking whom he may devour.*" As a Christian, you must know your identity in Christ Jesus, because the day you forget who you are in Christ and what He has done on Calvary's cross, the enemy will use this to his advantage. Christ became the curse for us, and before He died, Christ said, "It is finished." When Christ died on the cross, He reversed the curse, and we received redemption. In Romans 5:12–21, the apostle Paul offers us these words of hope:

Wherefore, as by one man sin entered into the world, and death by sin; and so death passed upon all men, for that all have sinned: (For until the law sin was in the world: but sin is not imputed when there is no law. Nevertheless death reigned from Adam to Moses, even over them that had not sinned after the similitude of Adam's transgression, who is the figure of him that was to come. But not as the offence, so also is the free gift. For if through the offence of one many be dead, much more the grace of God, and the gift by grace, which is by one man, Jesus Christ, hath abounded unto many. And not as it was by one that sinned, so is the gift: for the judgment was by one to condemnation, but the free gift is of many offences unto justification. For if by one man's offence death reigned by one; much more they which receive abundance of grace and of the gift of righteousness shall reign in life by one, Jesus Christ.) Therefore as by the offence of one judgment came upon all men to condemnation; even so by the righteousness of one the free gift came upon all men unto justification of life. For as by one man's disobedience many were made sinners, so by the obedience of one shall many be made righteous. Moreover the law entered, that the offence might abound. But where sin abounded, grace did much more abound: That as sin hath reigned unto death, even so might grace reign through righteousness unto eternal life by Jesus Christ our Lord.

Christians are not under generational curses. We have been bought with a price, through the work of Jesus Christ. (It was "paid in full.") Grace is God's unmerited favor. We must praise and magnify God for the things He has done, even before we existed. God has shown forth His love and His wonderful works He has performed for all humanity.

According to Galatians 3:13, "*Christ hath redeemed us from the curse of the law, being made a curse for us: for it is written, cursed is everyone who is hung on a tree.*" The enemy is deceiving people to think that they are cursed because of what their parents have done, but it is a lie. We must remember that we are not under the law, but we are under grace through Jesus Christ. Second Corinthians 5:21 states, "*For he hath made him to be sin for us, who knew no sin: that we might be made the righteousness of God in him.*" You are no longer a sinner: You may still sin, but you are not a sinner. Now we are the righteousness of God through Jesus Christ. The enemy will try to make you think that you are still a slave to sin, but we have received our freedom papers. We are not cursed people, but we are the blessed people of God.

4

What's in My System?

The body has many organs to run its systems, but if one organ fails, it will affect the rest of the system. But this is not the system that I'm talking about. What I mean is that what's in your system is causing you not to accomplish the things that God has placed in you. Let's look at the things that Israel has experienced that affected their spiritual system. Israel was made to worship the Egyptian gods. Israel was abused and was mistreated for over four hundred years, but I always wondered why Israel always wanted to return back to the hands of the Egyptians after all the things Pharaoh had done to them. You would think that after all of the things that God had done for the children of Israel, it should never have crossed their minds to want to go back to Egypt.

The apostle Paul let us know clearly what is going on with the Israelites: "*But I see another law in my members warring against the law of my mind, and bringing me into captivity to the law of sin which is in my members*" (Romans 7:23). The apostle Paul was letting us know that our war is against our minds. Israel was not only in captivity in Egypt, but they were also in captivity in their minds. Your old ways of thinking will affect your spiritual health. Many twenty-first-century Christians are in church, but they are still in prison in their minds. The sin that you see that is manifested on the outside, that is the sin that is at war on the inside. That's why, when you see a man or a woman go to prison and then they are finally set free from the justice system, we cannot understand why they would ever return to prison, but until you deal with what's in your system, you will return back to the system of sin.

There are many types of prisons in this world. For example, depression is one word but it has many symptoms—but depression is from the devil. It's a spirit of mind control, and we must put on the helmet of salvation, because Satan's target is to fill our mind with lies.

The enemy wants us to doubt our salvation. The helmet is meant to protect our mind from doubt, but there are many other spiritual sin systems that are keeping many people in captivity. Here they are at work: drugs, alcohol, tobacco, fornication, adultery, disobedience, lying, greed, homosexuality, arrogance, pride, selfishness, backbiting, unforgiveness, self-righteousness, suicide, fear, murder, division, prejudice, depression, bitterness, and anger. These spiritual sins affect both your physical and your spiritual health. As Christians, we are no longer under the sin system of Satan, but we are under the new system of Jesus Christ.

In John 10:10, Jesus reminded us that "*the thief comes only to steal and kill and destroy. I came that they may have life and have it abundantly.*" Your body is the temple of God where the Holy Spirit lives. With the help of the Holy Spirit, we must deny any access of an unclean spirit into our system. Proverbs 4:23 states: "*Keep thy heart with all diligence for out of it are the issues of life.*"

5

Keeping My Mind Out of Captivity

The enemy knows that whatever you let feed you will lead you. That is why we should never entertain our negative thoughts. That is the dead man trying to stay alive, and every opportunity that the enemy can get, he will take to try to catch the watchman off the wall of his mind. The enemy also knows that the mind is the driving force of decision-making: You are either going to make the right decision or the wrong decision. The apostle Paul explains what to do as watchmen on the wall of your mind: "*Casting down imagination and every high thing that exalted itself against the knowledge of God, and bringing into captivity every thought to the obedience of Christ*" (2 Corinthians 10:5). Starting today, stop letting your thoughts take you back to Egypt. What I mean is that every time you begin to do what God has promised you, what He has called you to do, you will always encounter spiritual conflict, either from the inside or from outside influence. The outside fight will always tempt us to become engaged in it, because we can see the war. This is when the enemy uses people to war against what God has promised you, on the inside. Second Corinthians10:3–4 tells us this: "*For though we walk in the flesh, we do not war after the flesh: (for the weapons of our warfare are not carnal, but mighty through God to the pulling down of strongholds).*" The real war is on the inside. The enemy is always trying to keep your mind in bondage. First John 4:4 states, "*Ye are of God, little children, and have overcome them: because greater is he that is in me, than he that is in the world.*"

The apostle Paul was able to see and understand the war within himself, but so many Christians around the world can only see other people's flaws. A mature Christian understands that the real war is not with human nature; it is with our flesh, the devil, and his fallen angels—and with himself. To get rid of stinky thinking, you must change the way you think, and one way to begin to do that is to pay attention to what you are listening to and what you are are watching and who you are letting speak into your life. These things will control your mind.

If you don't believe me, think of your mind as a television. We all know from watching television that it gives us a lot of choices with regard to information. Our television gives us images of the next big burger or the next new car, or luxury homes, or Victoria's Secret models, or divorce court, or many more things that are not listed here. What I'm trying to get you to see is that your mind is the same way: We have so many images bombarding us all day long, waiting for us to make a choice. The choice that I decide to make will determine whether I'm walking in freedom or in captivity.

In Romans 12:2, Paul wrote, "*Don't copy the behavior and customs of this world, but let God transform you into a new person by changing the way you think. Then you will learn to know God's will for you, which is good and pleasing and perfect will.*" The only thing that is keeping me from not knowing God's will for my life is what I'm thinking and the choices that I'm making. So, my mind must go through a metamorphosis, changing my old ways of thinking.

We say things about ourselves that are not the will of God for our lives, like "I'm not good enough." Our insecurities and fears—these thoughts play over and over in our minds, trying to keep us in captivity, but if we want a new mind, we must think on these things: "*Finally, brethren, whatsoever things are true, whatsoever thing are honest, whatsoever things are just, whatsoever things are lovely, whatsoever things are of good report; if there be any virtue, and if there be any praise think on these things*" (Philippians 4:8). So, I *can* know the perfect will of God for my life. In Romans 7:25, Paul wrote, "*Thanks be to God, who delivers me through Jesus Christ our Lord! So then, I myself in my mind am a slave to God's law, but in my sinful nature a slave to the law of sin.*"

If I'm going to win the war within, I must know who I am in God and what God has done through Jesus Christ. He has delivered me from sin! We must choose whom we will let rule (govern) us. I am subject to the things of God in my mind, but I must bring my sin nature under the control of the Spirit. In 1 Corinthians 9:27, Paul wrote,

"I keep under my body, and bring it into subjection: lest that by any means, when I have preached to others, I myself should be a castaway."

6

DON'T FIGHT IT, KILL IT

Whatever you do not kill, you will face again—just like the battle between Saul and Goliath. Don't fight it; kill it. God has called us to be giant killers, but the reason Saul could not kill the giant himself was because he was being disobedient to the God of Israel. Saul was still called; he was just no longer chosen by God. Although Saul was demoted, he continued to fight the giant Goliath in his own strength, without the help of God.

God is doing the same thing in the twenty-first century. God is executing demotion and promotion. The disobedient pastor will be exposed and a headship change will be executed by God in the church. We have to remember that nothing is hidden from God. Everything is an open book.

First Peter 4:17 states, "*The time is come that judgment must begin at the house of God: and if it first begin at us, what shall the end be of them that obey not the gospel of God?*" Saul was no longer walking in the will of God. Goliath represented the spiritual warfare that was coming against Israel, but disobedience will cause you to fight the evil things in your life for years but never overcome them. The enemy knows that the only power we have is the power of God through Jesus Christ. God then promoted and anointed King David to take Saul's position. Saul was trying to kill Goliath in his own strength, but David accomplished the killing of Goliath by walking in the power of God. It is the anointing that destroys the yoke of bondage, not our physicality or our pride or our influence. Only the power of God can do it!

As David entered the scene, from a human standpoint he was not the number-one choice, but the Bible clearly lets us know that man looks at the outside appearance, but God looks at the heart of men. That's why it is vital that we guard our hearts. Now, back to the twenty-first-century church: Jesus said in John 14:12: "*Most assuredly, I say to you, he who believes in Me, the works that I do he will do also; and greater works than these he will do, because I go to My Father"* (NKJV). The enemy is blinding the people of God with entertainment and other forms of pleasure, but God has called us to preach the Gospel all over the world, with power and authority—not with our own power, but with the power of God that He has invested in us. Disobedience will cause the old sin giant to creep back in your life, the giant that you thought was dead. Now it will show up at the peak of your ministry, but disobedience leaves you feeling completely uncovered. Remember: What you do not kill, you will face again. You can be a giant killer or a giant fighter.

You are called to bring down the giants of your generation. What is stopping you from moving forward? What threatens your destiny? We can't use Saul's tactics to bring down the giant because it will not be your flesh that will overcome the giant. Saul was preparing to go out to fight against the giant with all his armor and his soldiers, but he could not prevail. Why? Saul forget about the God who had called him to be king. Saul was self-centered and disobedient. This is an example from which every Christian and leader should learn. When God calls you to do something, you must do it His way. Proverbs 14:12 states, "*There is a way which seemeth right unto a man, but the end thereof are the ways of death.*"

You will never be able to bring down the giant while walking in the flesh. Your enemy will always have an advantage over you when you walk in the flesh. Your enemies will always be spirit-driven whether they are male or female. Saul was trying to fight the giants with his own strength and his position as the king. At this time, Saul only had authority in the flesh but not in the spiritual realm, because he had disobeyed God. God took back the spiritual authority He had given to Saul (the anointing). In Ephesians 6:12, Paul wrote that "*our struggle is not against flesh and blood, but against the rulers, against the authorities, against the powers of this dark world and against the spiritual forces of evil in the heavenly realms.*" Due to his relationship and his disobedience to God, God demoted him from being king over his people.

It is just like in churches today. Some are going through the motions without the promotion. You will not be able to function in a spiritual position without a relationship with God who called you to the position. In Luke 10:27, Jesus said, "*Love the Lord your God with all your heart and with all your soul and with all your strength and with all your mind.*" We should not love anything more than Him, not our position, our families, or our possessions. You are fooling yourself if you think that the enemy doesn't know the relationship that you have with God. Either we are serving God through Jesus Christ or we are serving our flesh, going through the motions, singing the songs, attending church every Sunday, but our hearts are not with Him, nor are we serving God in the spirit of truth, depending totally on Him to lead and guide us into all battles in all circumstances in our lives.

The enemy knows whether we are walking outside of the will of God. We are no challenge to the enemy—that is why Saul could not bring the giant down, because the giant knew that he had no authority to bring him down. Acts 19:15 gives us this insight: "*And the evil spirit answered and said, Jesus I know, and Paul I know; but who are you?*" Why would the enemy ask, "Who are you?" if you had some authority? It will never be your title nor your influence that brings down the giant. It is only through your relationship with God through Jesus Christ that you have any authority to bring down the giant in your life. Isaiah 10:27 states, "*And it shall come to pass in that day, that his burden shall be taken away from off thy shoulder and his yoke from off thy neck, and the yoke shall be destroyed because of the anointing.*"

Saul was able to fight the giant, but he was never able to destroy him because he didn't have the anointing to destroy the enemy that was opposing Israel. The enemy know who walks with the authority and the anointing of God. Mark 1:23–24 tell us that "*while Jesus was in the synagogue, a man was there that had an evil spirit (from the devil) inside him. The man shouted, 'Jesus of Nazareth! What do you want with us? Did you come to destroy us? I know who you are—God's Holy One!'*" (NIV). Jesus told the evil spirits to shut up and come out of the man. What I am trying to get you to see is that if you are living a life of obedience, the enemy must obey the authority of Jesus Christ and the anointing that rests on your life.

The reason Saul couldn't destroy Israel's enemy was that he failed to obey the voice of the Lord. Saul confessed this to Samuel: "I feared the people, and I listened to their voice." Sad to say, some of us are listening to the voice of the people in the twenty-first-century church. God did not call us to obey the voice of the people, but to obey *His* voice. Some of us are so scared to say anything to the congregation, fearing that they will stop paying their tithes, or not show up to church. Or they are scared that the people won't like them, or they are afraid they will be moved out of their positions, but if a leader walks in disobedience to God, the church will be in chaos and disorder. The enemy will have a field day at that church.

My prayer is that God sends some leaders with the heart of David into His vineyard, so that we will seek after God's heart, not seeking after titles and positions and influence and money. The anointing that God gives you will open up many doors, but your character will determine how long you stay there. God anointed David to do what Saul couldn't do: kill the giant.

Before David was anointed by God, he was building up his résumé. The two characteristics that we see is that David was spending time protecting and taking care of his father's sheep, David knew that it was his responsibility to protect his father's sheep, and at a young age, David was already showing leadership qualities. David killed a lion, and then he killed a bear. We see here that David's brothers didn't think it was of any significance that David was taking care of his father's small herd of sheep, because David's brothers were in the army. They felt that they were doing more than their younger brother.

Sometimes our position can deceive us, because while David's brothers thought what David was doing was insignificant, God was about to raise David up to be the next king. Remember that the first will be last and the last will be first. In Zechariah 4:10, God tells us, "*Do not despise these small beginnings for the Lord rejoice to see the work begin, to see the plumb line in Zerubbabel's hand. The seven lamps represent the eye of the Lord that search all around the world.*" When the Lord placed His anointing on your life, you were empowered with the DNA that holds the characteristics of God. Let no one intimidate you, because you don't have the degrees, or because people are overlooking you and choosing other people before you. They will know that God called you, by His Spirit resting on you. Jesus Himself said in Luke 10:19, "*Behold, I give unto you power to tread on serpents and scorpions, and over all the power of the enemy: and nothing shall by any means hurt you.*"

7

WHO'S TALKING?

There are so many spiritual voices in the world today. We have to be careful whom we let speak into our lives, who is speaking what, because if the enemy can use Peter's vocal cords, what do you think he will do with you or anybody else? Satan spoke through Peter to let Jesus know that he was not letting him go to Jerusalem to die. In Matthew 16:23, "*Jesus turned and said to Peter, 'Get behind me, Satan! You are a stumbling block to me; you do not have in mind the concerns of God, but merely human concerns'*" (NIV). The enemy's strategy was to use someone close to Jesus, because he knew that we will usually listen to the people who are closest to us, but Jesus' whole purpose and goal was to do the will of God. Anything that was outside the will of God made it easy for Jesus to recognize that Satan was trying to stop Him from fulfilling His purpose.

We have friends and family members who have spoken so many things out of their mouths that we didn't understand. We couldn't recognize that the enemy was using them, but after you read this chapter, you will have a clear understanding as to who is talking. I always tell my kids that if you ain't got nothing good to say, then don't say nothing at all. So, choose your words wisely. Words are very important, because God spoke everything into existence by the words of His mouth. Jesus knew how important words are, so when Peter opened his mouth and tried to stop Jesus from going to Jerusalem to die, Jesus knew that it wasn't the will of God for His life. That is why Jesus was born: Jesus came to die for the whole world.

Whatever the enemy has used to cause you to speak against yourself, whatever got you stuck in neutral, before you speak, pay close attention to your thought patterns, because whatever you speak is what you will become. Your mouth is your navigation system to your destiny, so whatever comes out of your mouth will create the direction you're going in, no matter whether it's good or bad. But the good thing about the life God has given us is that we can always reroute our lives by reprogramming our minds, so that when we speak, we will be speaking our destiny and not our destruction. The Bible clearly lets us know that the power of life and death is in the tongue, so you must use your mouth to your advantage to speak life. You have to speak how God thinks of you.

Jeremiah 29:11 makes it clear what God's plans for us actually are: "'*For I know the plans I have for you,' declares the* LORD, *'plans to prosper you and not to harm you, plans to give you hope and a future*'" (NIV). We must stop speaking negative things out of our mouths, because some days we do not speak the will God. Some days we feel uncertain and insecure, and we think that God feels the same way that we do, but God cannot never change who He is.

No matter what we feel, remember that God is not moved by your circumstances, but He's moved by your faith in your circumstance, so no matter what it looks like, "I am still an overcomer, through Jesus Christ!" You have to continue to speak this doing the good days and the bad days because God's Word never changes. Hebrews 13:8 tells us that "*Jesus Christ is the same yesterday, and today, and forever.*" That voice that you hear in your ear that keeps telling you that you're not loved, but it's a lie.

We must be careful whom we let prophesy into our lives. Many people are speaking things that God has not told them to speak. In Matthew 7:15 Jesus said to "*beware of false prophets which come to you in sheep's clothing, but inwardly they are ravening wolves.*" Jeremiah 23:16 states: "*Thus says the* LORD *of hosts, Do not listen to the words of the prophets who are prophesying to you. They are leading you into futility; they speak a vision of their own imagination, not from the mouth of the* LORD."

God is warning us about camouflage Christians. A camouflage Christian is someone who looks like you, sounds like you, and walks like you, but inwardly, they are nothing like you. Their motive is to win you over with their great speeches, so that you will think they have your best interests at heart. But all along they're trying to get you to trust them, and they will then cleverly teach you destructive heresies (2 Peter 2:1). The enemy will camouflage himself to be the light of God, so people of God, please pay close attention to what the Word of God has taught you.

If anyone comes confessing that Jesus Christ is not born in the flesh and does not confess that God raised Jesus from the dead, and if they confess that He is not the Son of God, this camouflage Christian is an antichrist. *Father, I pray that you will give the body of Christ the spirit of discernment and the spirit of insight so that they may see the enemy from afar off.*

First John 4:1 tells us this: "*Beloved, believe not every spirit, but try the spirits whether they are of God: because many false prophets are gone out into the world.*" You should know every individual by their spirit. Try it before you buy it. So many intelligent people are preaching—but preaching what? That is the question.

We as Christians must be discerning and test every word that is being preached and prophesied. Some have come into the world to deceive souls and not to save them, so test every spirit against the Holy Bible, which is the Word of God. God will never speak against His Word. The enemy will always camouflage himself to deceive you into believing his lies. Second Corinthians 11:13–15 tells us what is really going on: "*For such men are false apostles, deceitful workmen, disguising themselves as apostle of Christ. And no wonder, for even Satan disguises himself as an angel of light, so it no surprise if his servants, also disguise themselves as servants of righteousness.*"

Stop listening to people who are the servants of Satan. The only thing that comes out of their mouths are lies. Don't be fooled, thinking they are "safe" just because they are in church. Satan is in church every Sunday too! If a person is not fully committed to God, he will become Satan's vehicle, used to spread his poison of deception and lies. You must discern everything because it's not always what it looks like. Second Timothy 3:13 states: "*While evil people and impostors will go on from bad to worse, deceiving and being deceived*" (ESV).

Satan's helpers will not be able to camouflage themselves forever, and if Christians walk in the Word of our Lord Jesus Christ, we will always be able to recognize the devil, if we continue walking in the truth. As He has said, "Many will come and say 'I'm the Christ,' and many will be deceived." This spirit is sent to camouflage himself as Christ. Satan's purpose is to deceive many with signs and wonders and miracles, but it is all counterfeit.

We can see this same spirit running wild in the twenty-first-century identity theft. This spirit will always try to be what it is not. This spirit is everywhere—even when you go to the grocery store, as you gather all your groceries and proceed to check out, when you pull out a hundred-dollar bill to pay for your groceries, you may notice the cashier is examining your money. Why? Because she has been trained to identify counterfeit bills. If the world can identify fake money, the church must also be trained and warned in order to identify fake pastors and fake prophets.

What do I mean by "fake"? Mark 13:5–6 states: "*And Jesus answering them began to say, Take heed lest any man deceive you: For many shall come in my name, saying, I am Christ; and shall deceive many.*" Don't be fooled by what it looks like or what it sounds like This spirit has to be spiritually discerned, because it comes in different forms. Remember that the Lord has said that many spirits have gone out into the world. All of these spirits have the same purpose—deception—but different assignments.

8

Winning the War Within

The only way to win the war within is with the help of the Holy Spirit. Jesus was very clear that when He left to go be with the Father, He will send us a Helper—and that Helper is the Holy Spirit. In 1 John 4:4, God's Word tells us: "*Little children, you are from God and have overcome them, for he who is in you is greater than he who is in the world.*"

We can't win the war within without the Holy Spirit, because the Holy Spirit is our Helper. He will teach us all things—the things of God in the Spirit. We must monitor and choose what we will do or say with the help of the Holy Spirit.

Remember, it is our choice whom we will serve. In Matthew 6:24, Jesus said, "*No man can serve two masters: for either he will hate the one, and love the other; or else he will hold to the one, and despise the other. Ye cannot serve God and mammon (the flesh).*" That means we must make the right choices, but this takes a mature Christian who is led by the Holy Spirit to even know what is taking place within themselves.

So many Christians around the world have never discovered the war within. They are left wondering what is wrong with them. From one Christian to another, let me tell you that you are not crazy—you just haven't yet discovered your war within. In Romans 7:23, Paul described this conflict: "*But I see another law at work in me, waging war against the law of my mind and making me a prisoner of the law of sin at work within me.*" You are already a winner because of what Christ has done on Calvary's cross. It was because of the shedding of His blood that we can have a victorious life, but every day you must choose to win.

It is a mind-set. Romans 8:6 tells us that "*to set the mind on the flesh is death, but to set the mind on the spirit is life and peace.*" It is a choice that we must make. l choose to walk in the Spirit, the new man, with the help of the Holy Spirit. The Holy Spirit will bring all things back to your remembrance. It is vital that we study the Word of God, for it feeds the new man within. By fasting and prayer, the old man, the flesh, is weakened, and the new man is strengthened and we can reach our true potential. You must walk in the Spirit! In 2 Corinthians 3:17, Paul wrote, "*Now the Lord is the spirit, and where the spirit of the Lord is, there is freedom.*" Our freedom is in the Lord Jesus Christ.

9

Don't Take the Bait

Don't take the bait of the enemy—he is always trying to bait us and deceive us, but remember that every bait has a trap behind it. Make sure that your desires and your appetite are for the things of God. If not, it will be easy for the enemy to entrap you. First Peter 5:8 instructs us to "*be sober, be vigilant; because your adversary the devil, as a roaring lion, walketh about, seeking whom he may devour.*" Many of us have fallen victim to the enemy's bait of deception, but without discernment, it would be very hard to recognize the spiritual hook.

Remember, the enemy only shows you the bait that you desire. In James 1:14, we learn that "*each man is tempted when he is dragged away, enticed and baited (to commit sin) by his own (worldly) desire (lust passion)*" (AMP). Before a fisherman goes fishing, he first decides what bait to use, because not all fish like the same bait. The enemy knows this to be true for humanity. The enemy knows that if you are not a junkie, he will not be able to tempt you with drugs. We are only tempted by what we desire. The enemy has been using this strategy ever since the beginning, in Genesis, where he tempted Eve in the garden:

Now the serpent was more subtil than any beast of the field which the LORD God had made. And he said unto the woman, Yea, hath God said, Ye shall not eat of every tree of the garden? And the woman said unto the serpent, We may eat of the fruit of the trees of the garden: But of the fruit of the tree which is in the midst of the garden, God hath said, Ye shall not eat of it, neither shall ye touch it, lest ye die. And the serpent said unto the woman, Ye shall not surely die: For God doth know that in the day ye eat thereof, then your eyes shall be opened, and ye shall be as gods, knowing good and evil.

—Genesis 3:1–5

The enemy knows that the minute you disobey God with his deception, your life will never be the same. The enemy knows that every action has a reaction and every disobedience has a consequence. Adam and Eve were demoted from their spiritual relationship with God. Adam and Eve didn't even know they were naked, because they were more spiritually conscious than they were naturally conscious. But when Adam and Eve sinned, they became more naturally conscious. They were aware that they didn't have any clothes on. Sin will always strip you of your spiritual clothes and leave you naked and ashamed.

Adam tried to cover up what he had done, and he tried to hide himself from his Creator. God asked, "Where are you, Adam?" Adam said, "I was afraid and I hid myself, because I was naked." God said, "Who told you that you were naked?" They had a natural consciousness of their physical characteristics. God already knew that Adam and Eve had taken the bait of deception and had disobeyed Him.

Because of the choice of Adam and Eve, humanity was born into sin and man became sin-conscious. James1:14 tells us that "*each one is tempted when he is dragged away, enticed and baited (to commit sin) by his own (worldly) desire (lust, passion)*" (AMP). The enemy has been using the some bait of deception for over two thousand years. The strategy of the enemy is to discover what your appetite is, and once the enemy discover your appetite, then the enemy knows what he can bait you with—temptation.

The devil knows that he cannot use the same bait on every individual. Why? Because we all have different desires, so the enemy strategically watches for the symptoms of desire. Watch how the devil tried to tempt Jesus to sin. The same strategy that he used successfully with Adam and Eve, he tried to use on Jesus in the desert. The enemy knew that this was the Son of God because Matthew 3:17 tells us this: "*And lo, a voice from heaven, saying, This is my beloved Son, in whom I am well pleased.*" God had made an open announcement at the Jordan River that this was His Son.

Jesus had been fasting for forty days and forty nights, and the enemy knew that Jesus was hungry. Satan tried to use Jesus' appetite to get Jesus to obey him, but Jesus knew that He was not called to please His flesh, but He was to please God, His Father.

Jesus answered, It is written: Man shall not live on bread alone, but on every word that comes from the mouth of God. Then the devil took him to the holy city and had him stand on the highest point of the temple. If you are the Son of God, he said, throw yourself down, for it is written, He will commend his angels concerning you and they shall lift you up in their hands so that you will not strike your foot against a stone. Jesus answered him, It is also written, Do not put the Lord your God to the test.

—Matthew 4:4–6

Jesus' response to the enemy was with the Word of God. It is the same thing that Adam and Eve should have used and what we should use on a daily basis. So do not try to fight the enemy with your own strength—it won't work. You must fight the enemy with the Word of God—the truth.

So, don't take the bait. Even though everything the enemy tries to give to you will look good to your eyes, it won't be good for your life. The enemy only comes to assassinate your character. He will try to kill you and leave his seed of destruction and dysfunction in your life—so don't take the bait.

Unfortunately, many Christians have taken the enemy's bait unaware. Christians have taken the bait of infidelity, which has led to divorce, and it leaves dysfunction in a Christian home. The decision that one person makes doesn't just affect them, but it affects everything that is connected to that person. The enemy could be baiting you with your anger. The enemy knows you have an explosive temper, and the enemy knows that once you take the bait, your anger will not only destroy you, but it will also destroy the people you love. The enemy's whole purpose is to steal, kill, and destroy.

10

Let It Go

Israel wanted freedom, but they continued to hold on to their old baggage (Egypt). Before you can ever move forward, you have to be able to let your Egypt go. Egypt represents our past. I don't know what your Egypt is. What is causing you not to move forward today?

Egypt is the baggage of our past. We have all been enslaved at some point in our lives, either by our flesh or by the Spirit, and some of us are still enslaved by our past hurts and failures. We need to let this baggage go so that we can move forward in God. The enemy knows that if you choose to live your life walking in your past, you will never accomplish the things of God that He has planned for you.

Have you ever just been going through your everyday activities, when all of a sudden you have a flashback of your past hurts, and it rocks you to your core? It may feel like it happened yesterday, but it happened many years ago. The enemy uses this tactic to hold you in bondage.

Every time God was trying to move Israel forward, they always reverted back to bondage. Why is that? Because the Bible said it: "*For we wrestle not against flesh and blood, but against principalities, against the rulers of the darkness of this world, against spiritual wickedness in high places*" (Ephesians 6:12). Israel was worrying about the enemy that was in front of them in the Promised Land, but their biggest enemy was actually the spiritual influence by the enemy that was within them—the law of sin.

That is why we must let go of every negative thing such as anger, bitterness, and unforgiveness. Selfishness and a complaining spirit will always keep you in bondage. In Matthew 12:37, God's Word says: "*For by thy words thou shalt be justified, and by thy words thou shalt be condemned.*" Proverbs 6:2 tells us, "*You have been trapped by what you said, ensnared by the words of your mouth.*" Your mouth will play a great role into you moving into your next level.

Do you remember what Israel said when they were about to enter their promise? Israel said, "We are like grasshoppers." It was not what the enemy said about Israel that stopped Israel from moving forward, it was what Israel said about themselves. Israel felt inadequate.

Anytime you think that you have no purpose, you will never pursue your promise. Proverbs 18:7 states, "*A fool's mouth is his destruction, and his lips are the snare of his soul.*" When we are hurt and mistreated, we often feel that we have the right to put our pain and frustration center stage to let the world know about it, and so that no one else will ever hurt us again. Yes, it may sound good and feel good to our flesh, but we will only continue to live our lives in misery.

Bitterness is the root of it all. It is a venomous poison. Here are some of the symptoms of bitterness: unforgiveness, anger, pride, selfishness, and self-righteousness. We think that by holding on to the poison of bitterness, we are only hurting others, but we couldn't be more wrong. We are hurting ourselves, and we must let it go. Ephesians 4:31–32 tells us to "*get rid of all bitterness, rage and anger, brawling and slander, along with every form of malice. Be kind and compassionate to one another, forgiving each other, just as in Christ God forgave you.*"

We must get rid all anger and bitterness, because it will keep us in Egypt, still living in yesterday. We will never be able to move forward until we let it go. You would not believe how many Christians have been hurt by the church, but they are still holding on to that pain. You must let it go. I'm not saying that what they did to you was right—it was wrong! But you must forgive them so that *you* can move forward. In Matthew 6:14–15, Jesus said, "*For if you forgive other people when they sin against you, your heavenly Father will also forgive you. but if you do not forgive men their trespasses, neither will your Father forgive your trespasses.*"

11

PURSUE

We need to have Joshua and Caleb's attitude. They believed that they could have the Promised Land that God had promised them. Joshua and Caleb wanted to pursue and take the land. Joshua and Caleb believed God on the same day that God spoke to them that the land would be theirs, but the people didn't believe or have faith in God's provision. Anytime God gives you a vision, He always makes provision. That means that God has already prepared the blessing for you!

How long will you procrastinate doing the thing that God has asked you to do, so that you can receive what He has promised? What God places in you is not just for you; it is also for the world. Even when Israel was not actively pursuing God's promise, God's promise was still active. Although Israel was having issues, it still did not stop God from upholding what He had promised them.

For as the rain cometh down, and the snow from heaven, and returneth not thither, but watereth the earth, and maketh it bring forth and bud, that it may give seed to the sower, and bread to the eater: So shall my word be that goeth forth out of my mouth: it shall not return unto me void, but it shall accomplish that which I please, and it shall prosper in the thing whereto I sent it.

—Isaiah 55:10–11

God has not changed His mind, so that means you need to change your mind! Start pursuing your promise that is still lying dormant in you. It's time to stop sleepwalking and wake up to what God has placed inside of you.

I know the journey of life comes with many changes. Many of us have lost jobs or lost loved ones, or we have suffered addictions or divorce. But it still does not stop what God has placed in you. Through it all, the promise is still yours, so pursue it. Don't let yesterday's failures keep you from today's possibilities.

Jesus said unto him, If thou canst believe, all things are possible to him that believeth.

—Mark 9:23

That is the reason I said that we need to have the attitude of Caleb and Joshua. They never gave up on the vision. Don't think that just because God has promised you something, you won't have difficult times during the process.

Let me tell you about my difficult times—let me take you back about eleven years. I was at work one day, when all of a sudden I had a vision that I had three sources of income because of business deals. The vision was so real that it was like I was actually already there, prospering, but I was actually at work at my job. It was an out-of-body experience.

After I returned to work from my vision, I was so excited about what God was trying to do through me, but I did not understand the process of success. Everything took a drastic turn. 1 had worked four different jobs, but I never was able to receive financial freedom. Instead I as living from paycheck to paycheck, and the enemy came against my marriage. We went through so many trials and tribulations, and during that time, God sent my son to prophesy to me and my wife. He let me know that we were under an attack from the enemy, that he want to destroy our family, but that God would deliver us.

My son also said during the prophecy that I was a good starter but I wasn't a good finisher. I was excited about the idea of success but not the process it took to get there. Every time trials and tribulations came, 1 would stop the work.

Do you remember the spiritual side of Sanballat, Tobias, Geshem, and Arab? What I didn't understand at the time was that the vision that God had shown me was to help build up the kingdom of God. Every time trouble would show up, I would come down off of the wall of progress and the work stopped.

I thank God for Nehemiah—he give me the courage to keep on building, but Nehemiah faced the same thing when he asked the king to go and build up God's house. As soon as he began doing the work of God, here came the haters trying to stop his progress.

Nehemiah shows us what to do when we face opposition: Keep building! (See Nehemiah 6:1–3.) My son said one more thing to me, that God was about to bless our family financially. That was about two years ago, and since that time, everything has got better. I have started writing again to continue to pursue my promise.

One night my wife and I went to a five-night revival, and on the second night, the minister prophesied to me, saying, "I see four streams of income coming through you," but two weeks after the prophecy, my boss came to me and said, "You need to come to the meeting tomorrow at 10 a.m." I thought this would be a corporate meeting, but when I got there, it was only me and three other people: my boss, his boss, and the vice president. As I walked through the door, the vice president said to me, "I wish I had some good news to tell you, but we are letting you go." Remember, the minister had just prophesied to me two weeks before that four streams of income were going to come out of me. I could have been discouraged at the news, but I was at peace because it was time for me to pursue my promise. When one door closes, another door will open.

Second Corinthians 5:7 tells us, "*For we walk by faith, not by sight.*" When we face the pressures of life, it can cloudour vision, but it can never stop what God has promised you. Look at Joseph—when his father placed the coat of many colors on him. His brothers were disappointed in him because he had received the promise of his father.

So many times when God blesses us, the very people whom we think will be with us are the very people who are against us. Joseph's coat represented where he was going. His brothers noticed the favor and the calling on his life, and they were so disappointed that they decided to conspire against Joseph. It would be very surprising and hurtful to Joseph. When you discover who it is that doesn't want you to win, it will be painful.

Joseph's brothers were trying to stop his progress by putting Joseph in the pit of distress. The first thing the enemy tries to do when you begin pursuing your destiny is delay you and discourage you. Your calling is deeper than what you are going through at this present moment. Joseph was screaming for his brothers to help him. Joseph's brothers were able to help him, but they just didn't want to see him make progress into his destiny.

Romans 8:31 asks this question: "*What, then, shall we say in response to these things? If God is for us, who can be against us?*" To our human nature, it will seem impossible to make it without a supporting cast. The enemy will always use someone or something to distract you or try to keep you from pursuing your purpose. Why? Is the enemy fighting you so hard because you are the chosen one? Don't be surprised when people hate you—it's not that they hate you. They hate the calling and the favor of God on your life. So don't waste so much time trying to fit in, because you won't.

The gift on your life will cause people to misunderstand you. The gift of God on your life will cause people to think you have lost your mind. Who? Someone in your family will tell you that no one ever attempts the things that you are saying God is about to do in your life. If you look back on your family history and cannot see any reference of success, if the only thing you see are poverty and dysfunction and bad choices, this is why you were chosen. God is using you to rewrite your family history! And not only that, but He wants you to change the world.

First Corinthians 2:9 states, "*But as it is written, Eye hath not seen, nor ear heard, neither have entered into the heart of man, the things which God hath prepared for them that love him.*" Everything that you have experienced up to this point has been spiritually influenced by the enemy. As the saying goes, new levels, new devils. No matter what the struggle, no matter the forces that you are facing now, commit yourself to God.

Listen to the words of Psalm 37:5: "*Commit thy way unto the LORD; trust also in him; and he shall bring it to pass.*" You must continue to pursue your promise with tears in your eyes, and even when you don't understand what God is doing at this present time, pursue. When your family members turn their backs on you, pursue. The promise is yours.

ACKNOWLEDGMENTS

First and foremost, I would like to thank my heavenly Father for not ever giving up on me. God is truly faithful to His Word. Thanks to my wife, Shelly Depp, for all the scripture and her love and commitment for over thirty years. Thanks to the late Larry Tyrone Crawford Sr., for all the preaching and teaching that made an impact on my life to this day. I am the fruit of all of his labor. Thanks to Mr. Rhett Harwell, Trilogy acquisitions executive, for encouraging me to continue to move forward with the book. Thanks to Ta'Mara Gibbs, project manager, for all her hard work, working with the editor and the production team, helping to get this book accomplished. Thanks to Pastor Christopher Nubine for his encouraging words, and for being a true friend. Thanks to the proofreader. Thanks to TBN and Trilogy Publishing for their spirit of excellence, and for all of the hard work that it took to put this book together. God bless.

Epilogue

Uncover the strategy of the enemy against the saints and the people of this world. Jesus at the cross has given us our spiritual freedom papers. We are no longer slaves to the enemy of this world. The enemy knows that if you never discovered your true identity in Jesus, he can always bait you with his deception. Satan doesn't mind you having freedom papers. He just doesn't want you to live them out. There are so many Christians with their freedom papers but who live slavery lifestyles. Whom the Lord sets free is free indeed. No one can ever change what Jesus did at the cross, but until we make up our minds that we are kings with dominion, we will continue to be slaves to the system of this world. The enemy's philosophy is deception, to blind Christians from the truth. John 8:32 states: "And ye shall know the truth, and the truth shall make you free" (kjv). Truth is the key to freedom. The enemy hopes that he can keep us blind to the true reality of what Christ has done on Calvary's cross for humanity. The truth is that God wants no man to perish, but for everyone to come to repentance and the truth. Even in my own life, I have been deceived. I was anointed but immature. l didn't understand the power and the truth I was walking with, but what I didn't understand—that was where the enemy was going to test me. I didn't understand that I had to fight to keep my freedom. In John 10:10, Jesus tells us, "The thief only comes to steal, kill, and destroy. I came that they may have life, and may have it abundantly." I have had many trials and tribulations and failure. Not understanding who I am in Christ has caused me to fall victim to Satan's deception. Through Satan's strategy, his lies, and my lack of knowledge, I have disappointed God many times. This is my prayer to God every day: "God, help me be the man of God You have called me to be, even before I was in my mother's womb." I learned that one of the enemy's strategies is distraction, trying to keep me occupied with things that I see on the surface. Satan wants you to focus on problems, but not the promise, The problems are only coming because of the promise. What's the fight all about? The fight is about your future. The enemy never forgets what God has spoken over your life, so don't you forget what God has promised you. Just because it's delayed, it is not denied. Joseph had received a promise soon after the great announcement, The enemy within his brothers decided to conspire against Joseph, and the first thing the enemy did was to frustrate him and delay Joseph's promise by throwing him in the pit. The pit was not the promise. It was purpose. Anything that is going on in your life that does not line up with your promise, it is just purpose. According to Romans 8:28: "And we know that in all things God works for the good of those who love him, who have been called according to his purpose" (niv). The second thing that happened to Joseph that caught my attention was that his brothers sold him into slavery. This spirit will always try to keep you in bondage (Egypt). What the brothers didn't know was that they sold Joseph into purpose. Remember, whatever is not your promise is your purpose. I have learned that all the things I have been through in the purpose are to refine me. God was not denying me. You must be careful how you look at trouble. If you don't look at it right, you will say, "Why me?" But why not me? God will not call you out unless He is calling you into something great, causing you to go through a process. The process shows us who we really are in God, how much faith we have in God. We will face difficult times during our journey to freedom and prosperity. A poor mentality will cause you to live with a poor reality. When God brought Israel out of Egypt, He did not bring Israel out for them to keep the same mentality that they had in Egypt. What you don't change will remain. The enemy doesn't mind you going to church; he just doesn't want you to go through a metamorphosis. Roman 12:2 tells us: "Be not conformed to this world: but be ye transformed by the renewing of your mind, that ye may prove what is that good, and acceptable, and perfect, will of God" (kjv). I know that when we have new cars and houses and financial freedom, we think we have reached the pinnacle of success and freedom, Sadly this is not true, because if your mind is not free, you are not truly free. What keep us in Egypt is not our location, but it is our mentality. When God brings you out, it is to bring you in and to bring you to your destiny. When God brought the children of Israel into the wilderness, He brought them into the unfamiliar. God will always bring you into the unfamiliar, to do renovations on your old character. You cannot think the old way and receive the promises of God. In Matthew 9:17, Jesus said: "Nor do they put new wine into old wineskins, or else the wineskins break, the wine is spilled, and the wineskins are ruined. But they put new wine into new wineskins, and both are preserved" (nkjv). We must get rid of the old ways of thinking—bitterness, unforgiveness, unbelief—and lean not to our own understanding. This will keep our lives going in cycles, wondering and doubting the things of God. The promises of God are yours. The Bible says whom the Lord sets free is free, indeed. I have to feed my mind with the truth daily. God has brought you out of your personal Egypt, whatever that may be. Bit until you renew your mind, back to Egypt you will return with your freedom papers. There's nothing like a freed mind, because without it you will never discover the perfect will of God for your life. It is possible to go to church every Sunday, to pay your tithes and sing in the choir and preach the gospel. But our mind-set is conforming to the humanistic side: our emotions and our feelings and our daily thinking patterns that affect the perfect will of God for our lives. God wanted Israel to possess the land. It was God's will for them to possess it. Maybe someone was thinking, "Maybe God doesn't want me to have it." This is what I call the "lies of the enemy." This happens when I consistently think on the problem and not the promise. Proverbs 23:7–9 tells us: "For as he thinks in his heart, so is he [in behavior—one who manipulates]. He says to you, 'Eat and drink,' yet his heart is not with you [but it is begrudging the cost]" (amp). So many of us think out of our emotions and our feelings, but we must think out of the truth. The same authority that Jesus Christ demonstrated here on earth is what Christians should be walking in—the same authority and power. The devil still knows who the true believers are.

> God did extraordinary miracles through Paul, so that even handkerchiefs and aprons that had touched him were taken to the sick, and their illnesses were cured and the evil spirits left them. Some Jews who went around driving out evil spirits tried to invoke the name of the Lord Jesus over those who were demon-possessed. They would say, "In the name of Jesus, whom Paul preaches, I command you to come out." Seven sons of Sceva, a Jewish chief priest, were do-

ing this. One day the evil spirit answered him, "Jesus I know, and I know about Paul, but who are you?" Then the man who had the evil spirit jumped on them and overpowered them all. He gave them such a beating that they ran out of the house naked and bleeding.

—Acts 19:11–16

Does the enemy know your name in the Spirit realm? The seven sons of Sceva tried to drive out evil spirits in the name of Jesus without a relationship with Jesus. You are not a challenge to the enemy without a relationship with the Lord Jesus Christ, because Satan and his demons know who is walking in the power and the authority of the Lord. When Jesus was here on earth physically, He was our example, to show us our authority in the Spirit realm here on earth, Ephesians 6:12 states: "For we wrestle not against flesh and blood, but against principalities, against powers, against the rulers of the darkness of this world, against spiritual wickedness in high places" (kjv). Christians spend so much time fighting each other, not getting to the root of problem, which is a spiritual attack by the enemy. When Jesus was here on earth physically, every time He came in contact with an individual with an evil spirit, He always got to the root of matter, although it had a physical reaction. Jesus knew the problem was a spiritual condition.

> And in the synagogue there was a man, which had a spirit of an unclean devil, and cried out with a loud voice, saying, Let us alone; what have we to do with thee, thou Jesus of Nazareth? art thou come to destroy us? I know thee who thou art; the Holy One of God. And Jesus rebuked him, saying, Hold thy peace, and come out of him. And when the devil had thrown him in the midst, he came out of him, and hurt him not. And they were all amazed, and spake among themselves, saying, What a word is this! for with authority and power he commandeth the unclean spirits, and they come out.
>
> —Luke 4:33–36 kjv

We are tolerating the things of the enemy when we should be commanding him to come out. My relationship with Christ gives me the legal right to walk in power, but without a relationship with Christ, we are powerless against the enemy of this world. Through Christ's death and His resurrection, we are "more than conquerors."

> What, then, shall we say in response to these things? If God is for us, who can be against us? He who did not spare his own Son, but gave him up for us all—how will he not also, along with him, graciously give us all things? Who will bring any charge against those whom God has chosen? It is God who justifies. Who then is the one who condemns? No one. Christ Jesus who died—more than that, who was raised to life—is at the right hand of God and is also interceding for us. Who shall separate us from the love of Christ? Shall trouble or hardship or persecution or famine or nakedness or danger or sword? As it is written:"For your sake we face death all day long; we are considered as sheep to be slaughtered." No, in all these things we are more than conquerors through him who loved us. For I am convinced that neither death nor life, neither angels nor demons, neither the present nor the future, nor any powers, neither height nor depth, nor anything else in all creation, will be able to separate us from the love of God that is in Christ Jesus our Lord.
>
> —Romans 8:31–39 niv

Every knee must bow under the authority of Jesus Christ.

Scripture Notes

Introduction

And ye shall know the truth, and the truth shall make you free.
—John 8:32 kjv

The thief cometh not, but for to steal, and to kill, and to destroy: I am come that they might have life, and that they might have it more abundantly.
—John 10:10 kjv

And we know that all things work together for good to them that love God, to them who are the called according to his purpose.
—Romans 8:28 kjv

And ye shall know the truth, and the truth shall make you free.
—John 8:32 kjv

Chapter 1: The Wilderness

Neither do men put new into old bottles else the bottles break, and the wine runneth out,and the bottles: but they put new wine into new bottles, and both are preserved.
—Matthew 9:17 kjv

Trust in the Lord with all thine heart; and lean not unto thine own understanding.
—Proverbs 3:5 kjv

Do all things without murmurings and disputings.
—Philippians 2:14 kjv

Chapter 2: Faith Without Works Is Dead

What doth profit, my brethren, though a man say he hath faith and have not works? Can faith save him?

—James 12:14 kjv

Trust in the Lord with all heart; and lean not unto thine own understanding.

—Proverbs 3:5–7

Chapter 3: Generational Curses

Christ hath redeemed us from the curse of the law, being made a curse for it is written, cursed is everyone that hangeth on a tree.

—Galatians 3:13 kjv

Therefore if any man be in Christ, he is a new creature: old things are passed away; behold, all things are become new.

—2 Corinthians 5:17 kjv

For he hath made him to be sin for us, who knew no sin; that we might be made the righteousness of God in him.

—2 Corinthians 5:21 kjv

Chapter 4: What's in My System?

But I see another in my members, warring against the law of my mind, and bringing me into captivity to the law of sin which is in my members.

—Romans 7:23 kjv

The thief cometh not, but for to steal, and to kill, and to destroy: I am come that they might have life, and that they might have it more abundantly.

—John 10:10 kjv

Keep thy heart all diligence; for out of it are the issues of life.

—Proverbs 4:23 kjv

Chapter 5: Keeping My Mind Out of Captivity

Casting down imaginations, and every high thing that exalteth itself against the knowledge of God, and bringing into captivity every thought to the obedience of Christ.

—2 Corinthians 10:5 kjv

For though we walk in the flesh, we do not war after the flesh: (For the weapons of our warfare are not carnal, but mighty through God to the pulling down of strong holds).

—2 Corinthians 10:3–4 kjv

And be not conformed to this world: but be ye transformed by the renewing of your mind, that ye may prove what is that good, and acceptable, and perfect, will of God.

—Romans 12:2 kjv

Chapter 6: Don't Fight It; Kill It

Verily, verily, I say unto you, He that believeth on me, the works that I do shall he do also; and greater works than these shall he do; because I go unto my Father.

—John 14:12 kjv

And it shall come to pass in that day, that his burden shall be taken away from off thy shoulder, and his yoke from off thy neck, and the yoke shall be destroyed because of the anointing.

—Isaiah 10:27 kjv

And the evil spirit answered and said, Jesus I know, and Paul I know; but who are ye?

—Acts 19:15 kjv

Chapter 7: Who's Talking?

But he turned, and said unto Peter, Get thee behind me, Satan: thou art an offence unto me: for thou savourest not the things that be of God.

—Matthew 16:23 kjv

Thus saith the Lord of hosts, Hearken not unto the words of the prophets that prophesy unto you: they make you vain: they speak a vision of their own heart, and not out of the mouth of the Lord.

—Jeremiah 23:16 kjv

But there were false prophets also among the people, even as there shall be false teachers among you, who privily shall bring in damnable heresies, even denying the Lord that bought them, and bring upon themselves swift destructions.

—2 Peter 2:1 kjv

But he answered and said, It is written, Man shall not live by bread alone, but by every word that proceedeth out of the mouth of God.

—Matthew 4:4 kjv

Chapter 8: Winning the War Within

Ye are of God, little children, and have overcome them: because greater is he that is in you, than he that is in the world.

—1 John 4:4 kjv

But I see another law in my members, warring against the law of my mind, and bringing me into captivity to the law of sin which is in my members.

—Romans 7:23 kjv

Now the Lord is that Spirit: and where the Spirit of the Lord is, there is liberty.

—2 Corinthians 3:17 kjv

The thief cometh not, but for to steal, and to kill, and to destroy: I am come that they might have life, and that they might have it more abundantly.

—John 10:10 kjv

Chapter 9: Don't Take the Bait

Be sober, be vigilant; because your adversary the devil, as a roaring lion, walketh about, seeking whom he may devour.

—1 Peter 5:8 kjv

But every man is tempted, when he is drawn away of his own lust, and enticed.

—James 1:14 kjv

Now the serpent was more subtil than any beast of the field which the Lord God had made. And he said unto the woman, Yea, hath God said, Ye shall not eat of every tree of the garden?

—Genesis 3:1–5 kjv

Chapter 10: Let It Go

Let all bitterness, and wrath, and anger, and clamour, and evil speaking, be put away from you, with all malice.

—Ephesians 4:31 kjv

A fool's mouth is his destruction, and his lips are the snare of his soul.

—Proverbs 18:7 kjv

For if ye forgive men their trespasses, your heavenly Father will also forgive you: But if ye forgive not men their trespasses, neither will your Father forgive your trespasses.

—Matthew 6:14–15 kjv

For we wrestle not against flesh and blood, but against principalities, against powers, against the rulers of the darkness of this world, against spiritual wickedness in high places.

—Ephesians 6:12 kjv

Chapter 11: Pursue

Commit thy way unto the Lord; trust also in him; and he shall bring it to pass.

—Psalm 37:5 kjv

Now it came to pass, when Sanballat, and Tobiah, and Geshem the Arabian, and the rest of our enemies, heard that I had builded the wall, and that there was no breach left therein; (though at that time I had not set up the doors upon the gates;) that Sanballat and Geshem sent unto me, saying, Come, let us meet together in some one of the villages in the plain of Ono. But they thought to do me mischief. And I sent messengers unto them, saying, I am doing a great work, so that I cannot come down: why should the work cease, whilst I leave it, and come down to you?

—Nehemiah 6:1–3 kjv

What shall we then say to these things? If God be for us, who can be against us?

—Romans 8:31 kjv

CPSIA information can be obtained
at www.ICGtesting.com
Printed in the USA
JSHW041728041020
8457JS00001B/4